Lillian Fuchs

Fifteen Characteristic Studies

For Viola

OXFORD

UNIVERSITY PRESS

To Ludwig Stein

FIFTEEN CHARACTERISTIC STUDIES FOR VIOLA

I

Moderato ♩. = 112

LILLIAN FUCHS

Printed in U.S.A.

II

III

IV

V

VI

VII

VIII

IX

19

X

XI

XII

XIII

XIV

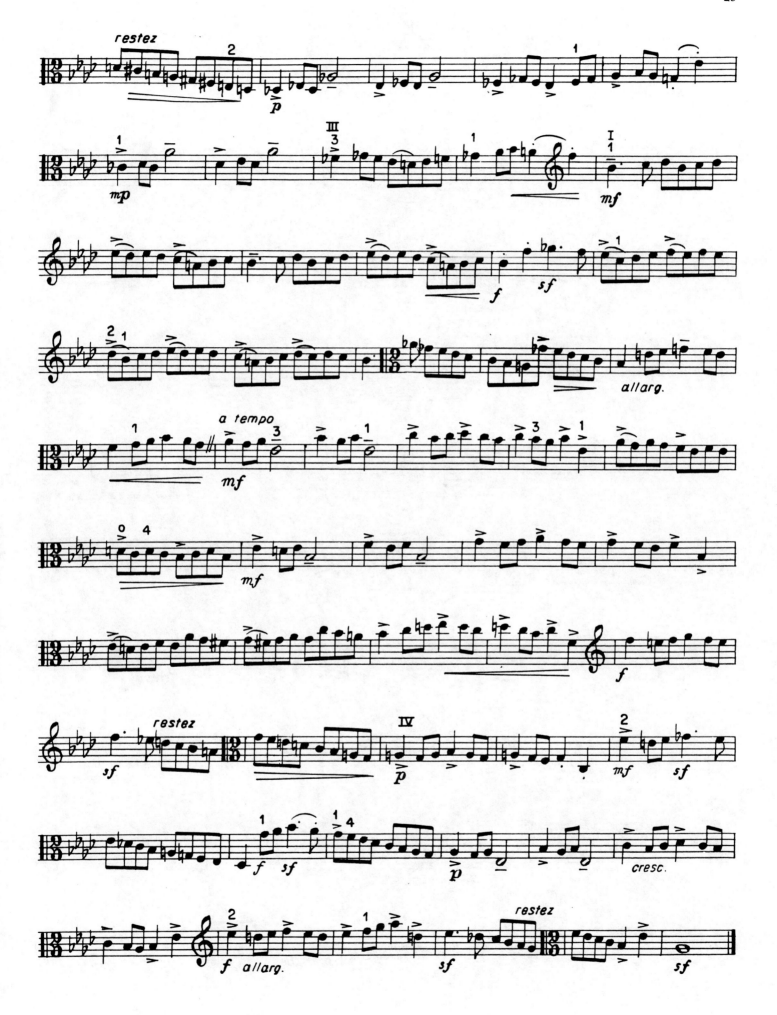

XV

PERPETUUM MOBILE